Legendary Warriors

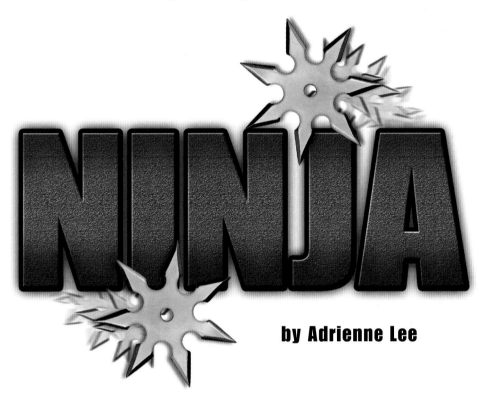

NINJA

by Adrienne Lee

Reading Consultant:
Barbara J. Fox
Professor Emerita
North Carolina State University

CAPSTONE PRESS
a capstone imprint

Blazers Books are published by Capstone Press,
1710 Roe Crest Drive, North Mankato, Minnesota 56003
www.capstonepub.com

Library of Congress Cataloging-in-Publication Data
Lee, Adrienne, 1981–
Ninja / by Adrienne Lee.
pages cm.—(Blazers books. Legendary warriors)
Includes index.
Summary: "Describes the lives of Japan's secretive Ninja warriors, including their daily life, weapons, and fighting techniques, as well as their place in popular culture"—Provided by publisher.
ISBN 978-1-4765-3112-0 (library binding)
ISBN 978-1-4765-3370-4 (ebook PDF)
1. Ninja—Japan—Juvenile literature. I. Title.
UB271.J3L44 2014
355.5'48—dc23   2013010454

Editorial Credits
Megan Peterson and Mandy Robbins, editors; Kyle Grenz, designer; Wanda Winch, media researcher; Jennifer Walker, production specialist

Photo Credits
Capstone Studio: Karon Dubke, 20 (bottom); Corbis: Michael Maslan Historic Photographs, 9; IGA-RYU Ninja Museum, 18; Image from Ninja AD 1460-1650, by Stephen Turnbull, © Osprey Publishing Ltd., 11, 12-13, 23;   Library of Congress: Prints and Photographs Division, 14-15; Newscom: akg-images/Werner Forman, 27, EPA/Abedin Taherkenareh, 28-29; Rachel Binx, 21; Shutterstock: 3dfoto, 20 (t), bigredlynx, back cover (sword), Boris Shevchuk, cover, 1 (shuriken), Dmitrijs Bindemanis, 5, Horimono, 17, Neale Cousland, cover (background), Ronen, cover (Ninja); SuperStock Inc: Culver Pictures, Inc., 24, DeAgostini, 6; Wikimedia: Samuraiantiqueworld, 19

Printed in the United States of America in Stevens Point, Wisconsin.
032013   007227WZF13

Table of Contents

ORIGINS OF THE NINJA

Surrounded by mystery, the ninja of Japan lived and fought in the shadows. These top-secret fighters formed in areas of Japan called Iga and Koga.

Most ninja were men. Female ninja were called kunoichi (KOO-nwa-chee).

IT'S A FACT

Some Japanese warriors who lost battles hid near Iga and Koga to avoid capture. Some of these warriors went on to become ninja.

The rulers of Iga forced farmers to pay high taxes. The farmers fought back many times. These farmers joined with warriors and Chinese and Korean **immigrants**. Together they created fighting skills called **ninjutsu**. Fighters were called ninja.

immigrant—a person who leaves one country and settles in another
ninjutsu—skills practiced by a ninja

Long ago, the **shogun** controlled Japan. He ruled the emperor's army. Sometimes the shogun lost power and control of the people. During these times, local rulers called **daimyo** fought to replace the shogun. Daimyo hired ninja to help them fight.

shogun—a military general who once ruled Japan
daimyo—a nobleman of Japan who owned a great
    deal of land

WAY OF THE NINJA

Japan's warrior class, the **samurai**, earned glory in battle. But ninja fought behind the scenes. Daimyo hired them to carry out secret missions. Ninja used unique weapons to carry out their jobs.

Ninja were feared because of their secret identities. Those who became famous were considered failures.

samurai—a skilled Japanese warrior who served one master or leader

identity—who or what you are

collapsible oar

grappling rod

water shoes

inflatable seat

flotation pots

11

Ninja taught ninjutsu to their
children at an early age. Children
learned to balance, jump, hide,
and run through mazes. Later
they learned how to fight with
their hands and feet.

As teenagers, ninja trained with weapons and learned how to spy.

Many ninja lived their lives in **disguise**. They pretended to be merchants and **monks**, traveling from place to place. They gathered information to prepare for sneak attacks.

disguise—made to look like someone else through clothes or makeup

monk—a man who lives in a religious community and promises to devote his life to his religion

TOOLS OF THE NINJA

Ninja mastered the skill of staying out of sight. They crept about in dark outfits of blue, green, rust, or brown. These colors blended well into many backgrounds. Sometimes ninja hid their faces with masks.

IT'S A FACT

Ninja often snuck into enemy castles and set them on fire.

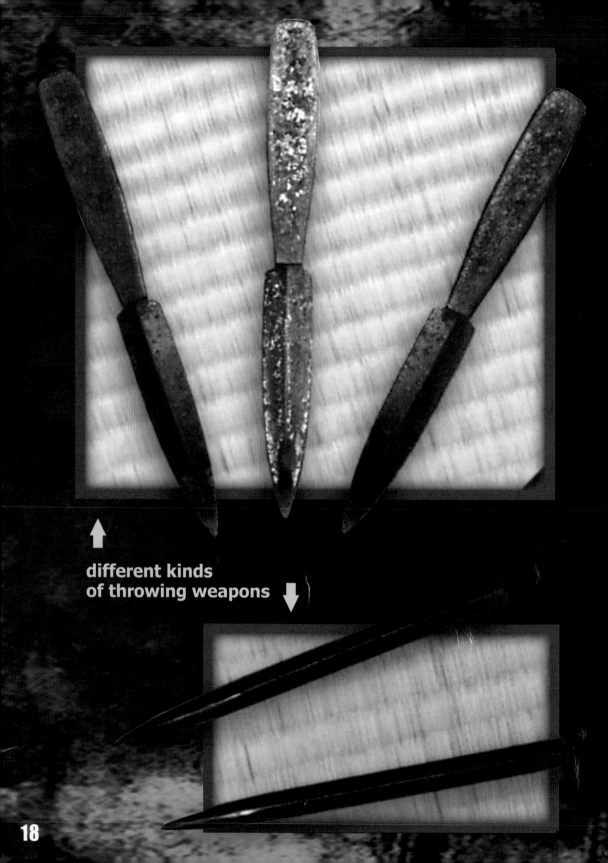

different kinds
of throwing weapons

A ninja's weapons had to be
easily hidden. Hollowed-out canes
held swords and knives. Ninja tucked
poisons and powders away in pouches.

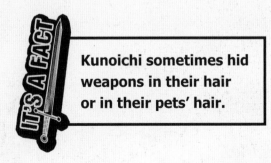

Kunoichi sometimes hid
weapons in their hair
or in their pets' hair.

To keep their identities secret, ninja ran away when they were attacked. When chased, they often threw star-shaped blades called shuriken behind them. Ninja used powder to blind attackers too.

Ninja snuck in and out of their homes using hidden tunnels and ladders.

THE NINJA FADE AWAY

In the late 1500s, a daimyo named Oda Nobunaga took over Japan. The ninja in Iga did not want to be ruled by Oda. Oda's troops attacked and defeated the ninja.

IT'S A FACT

During Oda's rule, many daimyo took ninja into their homes.

When Oda was killed in 1582, the men in his military began to fight for power. One man hungry for power was Tokugawa Ieyasu. He had taken in many Iga ninja. Now he needed them to repay his kindness.

IT'S A FACT

A ninja named Hanzo Hattori helped keep Tokugawa safe while he raised an army. Hanzo became a Japanese hero.

By 1600 Tokugawa controlled all of Japan. With no more fighting in Japan, the ninja were not needed. The ninja art of war faded away.

The Tokugawa family ruled peacefully for about 260 years.

Nijo Castle, headquarters of the Tokugawa family in Kyoto ➡

Today **martial arts** schools teach the skills of the early ninja. Even though students learn ninjutsu, they don't live like the ninja of years ago. Those mysterious warriors live only in stories from the past.

martial arts—styles of fighting or self-defense that come mostly from the Far East; tae kwon do, judo, and karate are examples of martial arts

According to legend, ninja first learned their skills from spirits called tengu. A tengu was half-bird and half-man. It lived in trees.

GLOSSARY

daimyo (DY-mee-oh)—a nobleman of Japan who owned a great deal of land

disguise (dis-GYZ)—made to look like someone else through clothes or makeup

identity (eye-DEN-ti-tee)—who or what you are

immigrant (IM-uh-gruhnt)—a person who leaves one country and settles in another

martial arts (MAR-shuhl ARTS)—styles of fighting or self-defense that come mostly from the Far East; tae kwon do, judo, and karate are examples of martial arts

monk (MUHNGK)—a man who lives in a religious community and promises to devote his life to his religion

ninjutsu (nihn-JIHT-soo)—skills practiced by a ninja

samurai (SAH-muh-rye)—a skilled Japanese warrior who served one master or leader

shogun (SHOH-guhn)—a military general who once ruled Japan

READ MORE

Guillain, Charlotte. *Ninja.* Fierce Fighters. Chicago: Raintree, 2010.

Malam, John. *You Wouldn't Want to Be a Ninja Warrior!: A Secret Job That's Your Destiny.* New York: Franklin Watts, 2011.

McDaniel, Sean. *Ninja.* Torque: History's Greatest Warriors. Minneapolis: Bellwether Media, 2012.

INTERNET SITES

FactHound offers a safe, fun way to find Internet sites related to this book. All of the sites on FactHound have been researched by our staff.

Here's all you do:

Visit *www.facthound.com*

Type in this code: 9781476531120

Check out projects, games and lots more at
www.capstonekids.com